# The Boom Bap Review

## VOLUME 1: 2019

MC TILL

MICHAEL STOVER

BEAU

ISBN: 9781089122678

# DEDICATION

Everybody's Hip-hop Label is a community-funded effort. This book would not have happened without the following (past &) present members of EHHL. If your name is not listed and you would like to become a member simply go to everybodyshiphop.com

We extend our utmost thanks to the following awesome people:

Akshay Wadekar
Andrew Whitton
Angelo Santoro
Brent A. Miller
Carlos Castillo
David Annett
Dee.kay
Derrick Braziel
Dhaval Kale
Elizabeth Koontz
Eric Hansen
Jarrod Alberich
Jay Whyle
Joe Thomas

Joey Taylor
John Stickney
Kenyon Turner
Kiff Kilpatrick
Mark Mcauley
Matthew Phillips
Michael Charron
Myrtis Smith
Nick Palermo
Robert Campbell
Spicey Ky
Taylor Hogle
Who Izzy

*- MC Till*

This book is dedicated to my Mom, my sister and the rest of my family. Without you I do not exist.

*- Michael Stover*

I dedicate this to Grandmaster Caz, Sylvia Robinson, and DJ Kool Herc.

*- Beau Brown*

# PREFACE

Remember when new releases came out on Tuesday? Remember when you could look in the back of *The Source* magazine to find out when your favorite artist was going to release their next album? Remember when Hip-hop used to be dope? Well, we believe all those things still exist. Dope Hip-hop music is coming out every week (except now, Friday is the new Tuesday). Instead of flipping to the end of *The Source*, you can get an email sent to you monthly with a list of dope Hip-hop that just came out, or is about to come out. Things have evolved, but as the saying goes, "The more things change, the more they stay the same."

Now, we won't go so far as to say Hip-hop in 2019 is better than, say, 1994. But, Hip-hop today IS dope, and it is part of our job at Everybody's Hip-hop label to make that case. As Black Sheep expressed back in 1991, "the choice is yours" whether you agree or not. So, we don't recommend you flip through this book in silence. Grab your phone or go sit by your CD or Vinyl collection, and get ready to search for some of the albums in this book. Get them out. Search them on Spotify. Play some music from them as you look back over another incredibly dope year in Hip-hop.

Enjoy,

MC Till

# TABLE OF CONTENTS

# INTRODUCTORY STUFF

This book is not a definitive list. In fact, we didn't even argue over this list of Boom Bap albums. I, MC Till, simply listed and wrote about my favorite albums from January 1st through November 1st. Albums released after Nov 1st are eligible for the Boom Bap Review in 2020. The albums I listened to and went back to repeatedly, I put in the top 25 and wrote about them. The other 75 albums are projects that I think are definitely worthy of your ears as well. So, I started working on this list and then my friend and co-manager at Everybody's Hip-hop Label, Michael Stover, comes along and says, "Hey, I want in on this action!" Done. We went back and forth and back and forth again and reworked the list. With two seasoned eyes and ears on the case, we think we have compiled some of the very best Boom Bap Hip-hop of 2019.

Now, let's keep a few things in mind. This book is not meant to cause a great schism in Hip-hop. Hahaha, as if we could create that. But it's not meant to create heated debate. We just love Hip-hop music and want to talk about it. We wrote this book hoping it will spark some conversation around the Hip-hop music that came out this year. We want to talk about the music and how good it is. Let's argue about the best in Hip-hop, not the worst. 2019 gave us plenty of great material to discuss.

Let us also keep in mind the phrase "Boom Bap." When we use this term, we are speaking primarily about the sound of the music. The "Boom Bap" sound as we understand it is all about the drums. Do the kicks hit hard? Are the snares loud and crisp?

Does the baseline pulsate in such a way that the neck just has to snap off? That's what we are talking about. BUT, and this is a huge but, we also let in several albums that might not necessarily fit this description. Common's new album *Let Love* might not fit it. Some of the newer drumless or less-drum-in-the-beats production might not fit. Yet, we include albums like that in the list. Why? Because this is Hip-hop. If we don't allow ourselves to break the rules from time to time, then we run the risk of not keeping with the spirit of Hip-hop.

Now, Michael and Beau are going to say a few words, and then we will jump in!

## *Michael*

Originally MC Till said a few words, so I only wrote a paragraph ...then I saw what Beau wrote so I'm rewriting this.

I've been reviewing music since about 2007 when my cousin gave me records from Sivion, Surreal and Braille. It changed my entire life as I had no clue that independent music was so different than what we were being fed on the radio.

Fast forward 12 years and my duty hasn't really changed, I'm just blessed to have people like MC Till and Beau who respect my expertise enough to work on a book together. This is a dream come true for me. You may not agree with some of our picks or the order, that's totally fine and ok, we want to start the discussion, there is no right or wrong answer. The idea is to introduce people to new music you might've missed in the hustle and bustle of life. The music landscape is insane these days as we enter 2020, every three days a new batch of records and instrumentals are being dropped. We hope this book will cause you to dip into some unknown territory.

Keep in mind that we want this to be a resource for you all. This isn't us saying these are the definitive top 100 albums of 2019. This is us saying here are 100 albums we enjoyed in 2019, maybe you haven't heard them, we enjoyed them and maybe you would too. If there are albums you would have in your 100, we'd absolutely love to hear them. Lastly, we're hoping to make this a yearly release and are already talking about changes and additions we want to make to the book. If there's anything you'd like to see, let us know as well!

My last random pitch in this introduction is to support the artists that you enjoy. Buy their records, attend their shows, buy their merchandise, I know you've heard this a million times before, but we're deep in a shift right now. Streaming is an incredible way to access your favorite music, however, I implore you to do a Google search and look at how much an artist makes per stream. It's less than a penny.

Buying music and products directly from the artists you enjoy allows and helps them to keep creating while supporting themselves and the families they're taking care of. Just something to think about as you read through. If you think you might like something, consider scooping up a CD or buy the digital album.

We really appreciate from the bottom of our hearts for buying the first Volume of our book series, without you none of this is possible.

## Beau

In 2006, when Nas released *Hip Hop Is Dead,* I thought he was right. Even though some great underground projects were dropping around that time, it seemed to me that the culture was becoming a thing of the past. "Everybody sound the same, commercialize the game, reminiscing when it wasn't all business," rapped Nas. As a lifelong guest in the house of Hip-hop, I felt like I was losing something integral to my existence.

Over the next several years, I continued to pay attention and listen. While many great things happening below the radar, nothing seemed to be bubbling up to the surface. Then, something happened. I'm not sure exactly what it was, but I can identify three turning points for me. In October 2012, Kendrick Lamar released *Good Kid, M.A.A.D. City*. Then, shortly afterward, February and June 2013 brought us *Czarface* and *Run the Jewels,* respectively. These three albums (which are now widely considered Hip-hop classics) sounded the alarm. Hip-hop is alive and well. (At some point, I'd like to delve more deeply into the circumstances surrounding this moment in Hip-hop, but MC Till and Michael Stover only gave me 500 words for the intro.)[1]

Since that time, there's been a steady, almost overwhelming, stream of excellent Hip-hop. Every week, we get multiple incredible projects from artists both new and established. Quite honestly, it can be too much to take in. It's difficult to set aside 3 or 4 hours every week to truly experience all this new music. Life gets hectic, and before you know it, you've missed several albums that you had been anticipating.

That's where the Boom Bap Review comes in. Our goal is to curate a list of important album releases that are continuing to shape the culture. We want to preserve this glut of content in a more substantial form that can be revisited again and again. In this age of ubiquitous digitized information, there's just something about a book you can hold in your hands. Any time you're in the mood for good Hip-hop, you can open this up to

---

[1] **Editor's note: MC Till and Michael Stover gave no such restriction.

any page, and we're willing to bet you'll enjoy any of the albums listed there.

In another sense, we want you to be able to put this up on your bookshelf or on your coffee table as an enduring piece of art in itself. Imagine the great conversations that will be sparked when people spot it on the shelf or pick the book up and start paging through it. Thanks to artist Phat Hentoff, the cover will be an eye-catcher for a lot of folks.

Whether or not Hip-hop was dead or dying back in 2006, it's definitely thriving now. At *Everybody's Hip Hop,* we'd like to keep it that way. Enjoy!

Part One

# THE TOP 100

(In order...

Well, the top 50 are an attempt to be.

51-100 are not in order,

but they are all dope!)

# Chapter 1: THE TOP 25

## # 1

## *The All*

### Smif N Wessun

Tek & Steele came back with a vengeance over production handled entirely by 9th Wonder & the Soul Council. Each beat hits hard with crackling snares, thumping kicks, well-placed high hats, excellent instrumentation, and heavenly sampling. While all that beauty is happening, the Boot Camp legends trade verses drenched in reflection, Islamic thought, and, of course, Brooklyn. Raekwon, Rapsody, Rick Ross, and GQ all stop by for stellar guest verses.

# # 2

## *Retropolitan*

### Skyzoo & Pete Rock

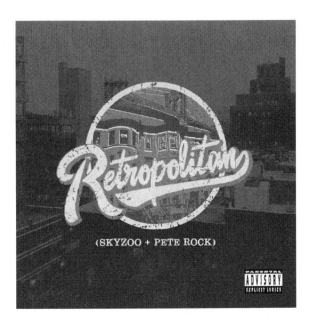

It seems as if Skyzoo can do no wrong when it comes to writing great albums. Pete Rock can do no wrong in producing them. Bring these two high-performing artists together and you get an excellent album in *Retropolitan*. The album feels great. Pete Rock provides his signature bass lines, horns, and overall dope sampling and sequencing while Skyzoo does what he does best: rap. This is a great album from two of the finest artists in Hip-hop.

## #3

## *Champion Sounds*

## Wordsworth & Pearl Gates

Lyrically, Wordsworth is sharper than ever while Pearl Gates holds his own with rapping bars and singing hooks. The production handled by Quincy Tones is cohesive, with Boom Bap drums and dope basslines tying it together. The music also features engaging melodies and catchy hooks that open the music to a wider audience while still holding a Boom Bap feel. That is no easy task, but these guys made it look so.

# # 4

## *Black Cesar*

### Knowledge the Pirate

Take one half Ka and mix it with one half Roc Marciano, and you get Knowledge the Pirate. His delivery is eerie as his voice has a staccato feel to it. It is totally present and confident while also sounding afraid or perhaps unsettling. Musically, *Black Cesar* is a triumph, holding space for every sample, each raw drum, and Knowledge's unique voice. Content-wise, the Pirate invites—no, demands—that you come into his world of drugs, extortion, murder, and more. It is dark and beautiful.

# #5

## *May the Lord Watch*

### Little Brother

Is 9th Wonder on the album? Might as well be, as the production is darn near flawless! But nope, Phonte and Rapper Big Pooh take fate into their own hands and find production outside of 9th. The two sound better than ever together, and they did a great job selecting the production. Skits reminiscent of *The Minstrel Show* run throughout the album, holding it together with their brand of comedy.

# # 6

## *Black Beans*

## Choosey & Exile

Exile & Choosey bring together the perfect blend of voice and beats. Choosey's lyrics and delivery are on point, but his voice is what really jumps out as it flows so smoothly over Exile's production. The beats are classic Exile—probably not better than *Below the Heavens* but not far off. This is an excellent album all the way through.

# # 7

## *Secrets & Escapes*

## *Brother Ali*
### *(Produced by Evidence)*

Without any marketing, these two living legends just up and dropped a dope album toward the end of the year. Maybe they knew the music would speak for itself. It does. Evidence delivers some of his best production to date. The beats are slow-moving, grimy with a touch of soul, traditional Boom Bap mixed with just a little new school lo-fi. Brother Ali continues his run as one of the most consistent lyricists spitting nothing but dopeness.

# # 8

## *Rise of Da Moon*

### Black Moon

It has been nearly two decades since Black Moon released an album. Do they still have it? Yes. Evil Dee doesn't try to switch up his style at all. He comes with underground Boom Bap beats on every track. Buckshot comes across super chill on almost every track, even getting his sing-song style on. To balance things out, 5 ft comes in with plenty of aggression and energy in his delivery. The two sound great together, and they don't need any help. Still, they get great appearances from Tek, Steele, Method Man & the Rockness Monsta.

# # 9

## *Transportation* + *It Wasn't Even Close*

## **Your Old Droog**

Your Old Droog released *It Wasn't Even Close* in April, turned around and released *Transportation* in June. Both projects are classic YOD material and are pretty much on the same level. I like *Transportation* more because I like the production on it slightly more than *It Wasn't Even Close*. Ironically, it was very close though!

# # 10

## *Sincerely, Detroit*

## Apollo Brown

Apollo Brown sticks to the script: dope soul chopped sampling with hard hitting drums. It works again! This time, he trades in the solo emcee format for hundreds of Detroit rappers! Haha. Okay, it is only around 50 Detroit artists. Still, that's a lot of rappers on one album. But being that they are all from Detroit and all pay homage in their own way to the Motor City, it works. It works really well. It is soulful, lyrical, and straight up Boom Bap Hip-hop! The only thing missing from this album is the presence of Eminem. It is an album featuring all Detroit rappers after all. But honestly, it is probably best this way. If Em was on the album, you know we would all be arguing about whether his song was the best or the worst!!!

# # 11

## *One of the Best Yet*

### Gang Starr

Word is DJ Premier had to pay a pretty large ransom for the lost Guru vocals, but he got them, reworked them, and gave us another Gang Starr album. Posthumous albums are hard and rarely work well. This is an exception. Several of the songs sound like Guru was right there recording to those beats. The features are cool too, as Premier rounded up the original Gang Starr Foundation and brought in heavyweights like Q-Tip, MOP, Royce and more. The production is pretty dope too. DJ Premier offers some great head-nodding beats to tie it all together. One of the best yet? Indeed.

# # 12

## *Logistix*

## Ill Conscience

This album is pure mid-90s east coast Boom Bap bliss. It has all the elements from that era: from the samples to the drums to Ill's stream-of-consciousness, lyrical wizardry delivery. It is all there, and the album never deviates from this formula. The consistent cohesion throughout this album is delicious.

# # 13

## *That's the World*

### Anti-Lilly & Phoniks

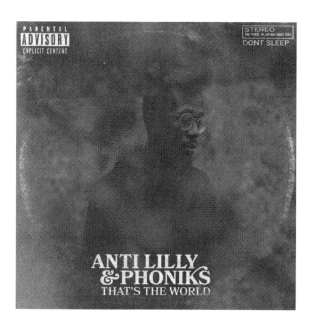

On the second track, "Don't (It) Feel So Good," Anti-Lilly opens up with a faint adlib "It feels so good." That pretty much sums up this album. It is incredibly jazzy and fresh but in a very subtle way. It does feel so good as Phoniks provides some of his best laid-back jazzy & soul-infused Boom Bap yet, and Anti-Lilly gets vulnerable song after song with a very gentle but fully present delivery.

# # 14

## *Let Love*

## Common

Hold on. I know what you are saying. "This isn't Boom Bap." Technically, you are correct, but Boom Bap elements do run throughout. You know you hear a little boom in that muffled Jay Dilla kick in "HER love." Songs like "Forever Your Love," "Memories of Home," and "God is Love" certainly don't scream Boom Bap on first listen, but step back for a moment. Go back and listen to each of those songs. Imagine replacing the soft pianos and strings for a chopped up sample like something DJ Premier would provide. Now, tell me that wouldn't be Boom Bap! The boom and the bap are present in the drums on many joints from *Let Love*, if you will let yourself hear it.

And so what if we disagree over the Boom Bap description? Yes, this book is the Boom Bap Review, so it is logical that we present albums that fit that description. But this is Hip-hop. Let us never forget that. Hip-hop broke rules. Hip-hop went against the culture. Hip-hop didn't sit around and wait for everyone to get on the same page. Hip-hop lived. It breathed. It started as a borough phenomenon and expanded throughout the globe.

And here we are, decades later, advancing the music, the conversation, the movement. We don't have to agree on everything. If you say *Let Love* is the farthest thing from Boom Bap and we say different, then that's just fine. We can disagree and well, hmmm, I guess just let love :)

# # 15

## *The Iliad Is Dead and the Odyssey Is Over*

## Murs

Seems as if 9th Wonder & The Soul Council can do no wrong in 2019. Could this be Murs' best work yet? It just might be. The production is on point throughout, and it has a very Boom Bap consistency. Lyrically, Murs does what he does: solid rhyming with a commanding presence on the mic.

# #16

## *Bandana*

### Freddie Gibbs

I love the juxtaposition of gangster rapper meets underground obscure sample-using head. Gibbs has a really dope voice, and he raps that rappity rap type rap. Both elements sound lovely over Madlib's jazz-funk-soul laced production. *Bandana* is a fun listen from beginning to end as beat-changes run rampant and Gibbs raps gangsta tales mixed with a little reflection sprinkled sparingly.

# # 17

## *Hell's Roof*

## Eto & DJ Muggs

Rhetorical question here, but you are welcome to answer it: "Can DJ Muggs do no wrong?" I promise he has been on a rampage of providing dope, underground, off-kilter, dark production to street savvy emcees. This project with Eto is no exception and might be Muggs' finest work in recent years. Eto's voice and street content mixes beautifully with Muggs' eerie production.

## #18

## *A Long Red Hot Los Angeles Summer Night*

## Blu & Oh No

Oh No provides summertime production for Blu to paint a picture of… you guessed it *A Long Red Hot Los Angeles Summer Night*. This album features dope lyricism and dope production. It also features a dope concept. One can go back to the album again and again for all these different reasons. Each play feels as fresh as the previous. It is a great musical, as well as literary, work.

# #19

## *TwoFive to Jersey*

## $wank & King Draft

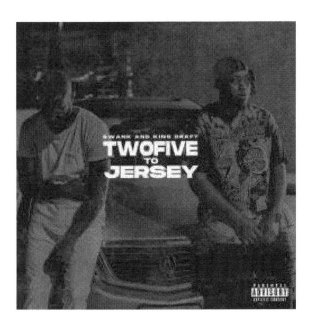

Full disclosure: we don't know who $wank & King Draft are. Don't know where they came from. All we know is that, out of seemingly nowhere, this album *TwoFive to Jersey* came out on Jamla. We imagine 9th Wonder and the Soul Council produced it because it sounds that way. Thick drums and soulful samples give $wank and King Draft the perfect soundbed to sound off. They have an old school feel that's fun. We hope to hear more from them.

# # 20

## *TrillStatik*

### Bun B & Statik Selektah

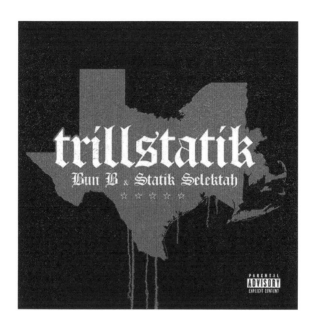

I absolutely love Bun B when he raps over Boom Bap production. His cadence and presence on the mic are in a lane of their own. Statik Selektah comes through with that kind of production, and they invite a host of emcees to join the party. Plus, if the music isn't enough, you can watch the entire recording process as they live-streamed the session.

# #21

## *Ground & Water*

## Blu & Damu the Fudgemunk

Classic Blu delivery over vintage 90s-influenced production from Damu the Fudgemunk. What more can one ask for? Perhaps more of just that. The only critique of this album is its brevity. However, an 8-song project in 2019 is pretty good. What's better, this little album packs nostalgic Boom Bap vibes from start to finish.

# # 22

## *Soulapowa*

## Awon

Awon spits straightforward lyrics over excellently-selected Boom Bap production. Phoniks produces half the album while Linkrust, Dread Solo, Soul Chef, and Dugga contribute one track each. One of the beats comes from Mz Boom Bap with "Lotor." Trust us. Put it on, grab something smooth to drink and enjoy one of the best Boom Bap albums of the year (I guess the 22nd best, in our opinion).

# # 23

## *Sincerely, The P*

## People Under the Stairs

The last album from PUTS is another stellar mixture of fun lyrics and dope beats. Did these guys ever put out a wack album? Maybe some were better than others, but they always came through with great music. *Sincerely, the P* is no exception. Thanks for all the good times, fellas. We appreciate your dedication to the craft. We will miss you.

# # 24

## *86 Witness*

## Sean Price & Small Professor

What do you expect? It is Sean Price. Enough said. Rest in **P**eace. Okay, we'll say more. If you don't know Sean Price, well then you probably picked this book up off the shelf of someone else's home. Put it back or pull a Sean Price move and steal it. Then, go listen to Sean Price. More than likely, you know Sean Price. You might not know Small Professor. Please get to know him. His sample-based Boom Bap production is always on point! It matches perfect here with Sean P's delivery. Guests include Quelle Chris, Rock, Guilty Simpson, Your Old Droog, and more.

# # 25

## *The Plugs I Met*

## Benny the Butcher

Griselda can do no wrong right now with their blend of eerie sample-based beats and street tales. This album is proof. Play the first song on this joint, "Crowns for Kings," and hear Benny the Butcher sound right at home with arguably the greatest rapper out right now, Black Thought. You've probably heard the sample in that song before, but listen to the energy in it with Benny behind it. Feels doper than ever. Album starts off with a bang and remains powerful throughout.

# CHAPTER 2: ALBUMS 26 – 50

## # 26
## *Here's Mud In Your Eye*
## Krum & Theory Hazit

Theory Hazit brings some of his best Boom Bap head nodding production to date. KRUM meets those beats with some of his best lyrics of his career.

## #27
## *A.G.E.*
## Planet Asia

Just give this man dope beats, and he makes incredible Hip-hop every time. And that's exactly what happened on A.G.E.

## # 28
## *Drum Machine Tape Cassette*
## Kev Brown & J Scienide

Underground. Original. Samples. Dust. Soul. Heart. Heaven. Pen & Pad. Vinyl Records. Lyricism. Hip-hop.

# # 29
## *Yuck!*
## **Anoyd & Statik Selektah**

Anoyd flows effortlessly over Statik's jazzy Boom Bap production.

# #30
## *Wap Konn Jòj!*

## *Tuez-Les Tous*
## **Mach-Hommy**

Mach's voice sounds great over grimy (Tuez) & jazzy beats (Wap).

# #31
## *Gorilla Monsoon*
## **Nems**

Take some classic breakbeats, grab some classic samples, and mesh them together in a new, exciting way and bring in an emcee for a lyrical mass murder spree, and you get this album. Classic breakbeats plus classic samples X lyrical mass murder

spree = this album

## #32
### *City for Sale*
### Von Pea

Von Pea brings the funk on this self-produced album. Upbeat beats meet fun, inviting lyrics for perhaps Von Pea's best album to date.

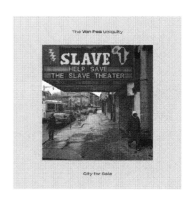

## #33
### *Mind of a Man*
### Justo the MC & Maticulous

Excellent blend of dope underground beats by Maticulous matched with mature rapping and rugged singing from Justo the MC makes this a great New York Boom Bap album.

## #34
### Sportee
### Nolan the Ninja

This dude can rap his butt off. And he does so on every song, over lo-fi Boom Bap beats. Dope.

## #35
## *A Bullet for Every Heathen*
## 38 Spesh & Big Ghost Ltd

Big Ghost Ltd comes through with some incredible soul singing production and 38 Spesh does what he does: grimy street poetry.

## #36
## *Czarface Meets Ghostface*

Ghost is as hungry as ever, rapping alongside Inspectah Deck & Esoteric over gritty, dark samples and sometimes-subtle drums provided by the Czarkeys.

## #37
## *Guns*
## Quelle Chris

The quirky emcee returns for another adventure through space and sound and guns. If you like Quelle Chris, you'll love it. Don't know who he is? Give him a shot. (pun not intended)

## #38
## *Lost Tapes II*
## Nas

Nas switches up his style a bit here and there over pretty solid production. Even Nas's misses are dope.

## #39
## *Eve*
## Rapsody

Over eclectic production, Rapsody pays homage to women with her signature flow that sounds as good as ever.

## #40
## *Ghostface Killahs*
## Ghostface Killah

Ghostface is back once again with another solid project. Storytelling and talking ish over dope production is classic Ghostface.

# #41
## Statue of Limitations
## Benny the Butcher, Smoke DZA, & Pete Rock

Short but packs a big bite. Benny & Smoke trade verses over dope Pete Rock production. Also features Conway, Westside Gunn, & Styles P.

# #42
## *Dusty*
## Homeboy Sandman

Homeboy Sandman is something out of this world. How he makes all those words work in that order with that cadence is incredible. Production is on point too.

# #43
## *Yacht Rock 2*
## Alchemist

Okay, so this isn't really Boom Bap, but dang, it's dope! Take a quick break from the Boom Bap and play this laidback masterpiece.

# #44
## *Actus Reus*
## Guilty Simpson

Guilty sounds dope as ever over soulful yet grimy production from Dixon Hill.

# #45
## JayARE
## *Youth Culture Power*
## (J Rawls & John Robinson)

Dope beats. Dope rhymes. Dope cause. What else can you ask for? More!

# #46
## *One Word, No Spaces*
## Donwill

Funky, Boom Bap beats set up Donwill to deliver a dope album. He                  does.

# #47
## *Wet Dirt*
### Crimeapple & DJ Skizz

It is beautiful and raw and soulful all mixed into a wonderful musical mosaic.

# #48
## *Chamber No. 9*
### Inspectah Deck

Lyrically, Deck can do no wrong. On *Chapter No. 9*, he is met with pretty dope production, giving him two projects in the top 50 just like his Wu partner Ghostface.

# #49
## *Complicate Your Life with Violence*
### Jeremiah Jae & L'Orange

L 'Orange comes with that 50s-sample Boom Bap, and Jeremiah Jae sounds brilliant.

## #50
## *Magma*
## Ruste Juxx & Tone Spliff

This album is its title: Magma. It is hard Hip-hop: Rough, rugged, n raw.

## CHAPTER 3: ALBUMS 51 – 100

Okay, we put the first 50 in the best order we could. Remember, this is all opinion. Now, with 51-100, we will simply list the albums without worrying about order. We think all of these projects are dope. Let's get to listing…

### *Planted Seeds*
### EL Maryacho

### *Holy Grail*
### Napoleon Da Legend

### *The Proletarii*
### GRIM MOSES

### *Monday*
### Haz

## *Cigarettes & Coffee*
### A.J. Munson

## *Gran Turismo*
### Curren$y & Statik Selektah

## *Take Everything*
### Live Percenters

## *Boulevard Author*
### Showbiz & Milano

## *Soul On Ice 2*
### Ras Kass

## *Cannibal Hulk*
### Ill Bill & Stu Bangas

## *Ace Balthazar*
### Beans

## *Popular Mechanics*
### Bozack Morris & J. Scienide

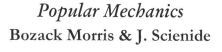

## *Initials On My Jewelry*
### Planet Asia

## *Vernia*
### Erick Sermon

## *The Unfortunate Case...*
### Moses Rockwell

## *The Big Kill*
### Killy Shoot

## WORD
### Rob Cave & The Other Guys

## FLYPM II
### Da Fly Hooligan

## Tell Your Uncle
### PENPALS X Junclassic

## Good for Nuthin
### The Good People

## Monday
### Joell Ortiz

## STAR TRUTH
### THA GOD FAHIM

## Heather Grey
**V Don X Willie The Kid X Eto**

## Forever Queens
**Starvin B & Discourse**

## 88 To Now
**Sareem Poems & Newselph**

## Black Ninjutsu
**Kyo Itachi & Haile Ali**

## Terror Management
**Billy Woods**

## uknowwhatimsayin?
**Danny Brown**

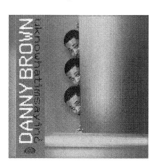

## The Between Time EP
### Ozay Moore

## Adventures of a Reluctant Superhero
### Chali 2na & Kraft Kuts

## Power of the Mind
### A.C. The Entity

## Social Meteor Vol. 1
### Es

## The Donner Party
### Deca & Neon Brown

## CRYPTEX
### Al Divino | Raticus

## *A Different Crown*
### Rel McCoy

## *Hitler Wears Hermes 7*
### Westside Gunn

## *Room 39 Part 2*
### Ty Farris

## *Reign Supreme*
### ANKHLEJOHN

## *RocAmeriKKKa*
### Eto x Flee Lord

## *Nomads*
### XP The Marxman & Ice Rocks

## Clark Connoisseurs
**Supreme Cerebral & Eloh Kush**

## KWESBAAR
**Neak**

## SLIME Wave
**Hus Kingpin**

## Thought Instruments
**Learic & Es-K**

## The Thrill of the Hunt 2
**Che` Noir**

## Still
**Clear Soul Forces**

## *Out to Sea*
### Chris Orrick

## *The Book of Cyphaden*
### Taiyamo Denku

## *Cipher*
### Nomad Carlos & Farma Beats

## *Ardore Melodico*
### Tone Spliff

## *Don't Eat the Fruit*
### Elcamino

## *Funhouse Mirror*
### Marlon Craft

## *ScienZe Was Here*
### ScienZe

## *Sacrifice EP*
### Supastition

## *Holly Water*
### Fly Anakin & Big Kahuna OG

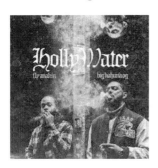

# Honorable Mentions

*Summer Classics* - Bobby J from Rockaway

*Let the Sun Talk* – Mavi

*From the Soul* – Revolutionary Rhythm

*Pensieve* – Dex Amora & Goldenbeets

*Emergency Raps, Vol. 4* – Fly Anakin & Tuamie

*Guest Room 2* – Cas Metah

# Parting Thoughts

Okay, that's the list. And if you do the math, you'll see that we couldn't keep it to just 100. There are actually 105 albums included here. There's so much good music out there that we had to make space for some extras…and then some honorable mentions on top of that.

Still, you might be thinking we left someone off, didn't rank a certain album high enough, or put an album way too high. This is Hip-hop so of course we can have that discussion. However, this list is what we like, not necessarily what we think is the best analytically. So, what do you think? Dig the list? Heard about some new albums? Just can't let go of the fact that we have _____ (insert album name) at number _____ (insert ranking). Well, let us know! We let you know what we think is dope, now you tell us what you think is dope! Drop us an email at adam.hayden.618@gmail.com or shoot us a text at 812-430-4464.

# ADDITIONAL STUFF

Now that you took a break to give us a piece of your mind, let's move into some extended writing about several albums this year as well as a few anniversary pieces from 25, 20, 15, and 10 years ago. Most of our writing here should feel consistent to our style of describing the music and writing how we experience it. So, pick one of those 100 albums we just walked through, put it on in the background, and enjoy some Hip-hop on paper.

Part Two

# LONG-FORM REVIEWS

# CHAPTER FOUR
## *The All* - Smif N Wessun
### Written by MC Till

I was at the record store sometime around the summer or fall of 1995. I saw two CDs in the used section that I wanted: "2000" by Grand Puba and "Dah Shinin" by Smif-N-Wessun. Luckily, I had enough money and bought both of them from Coconuts Record Store in Evansville, IN.

I liked Grand Puba's album just fine, but it was "Dah Shinin" that really inspired me. I could not relate to their lyrical content, but I could listen, and I did. I listened to Tek & Steele describe what life was like for them and their community in Brooklyn, NY. That was fascinating.

What struck me the most about that album was the music and the way the two emcees traded bars back and forth. The musical landscape, crafted by the Beatminerz, was like mixing early Mobb Deep and Tribe Called Quest. It had a very dark feel like Mobb and a smooth, almost jazzy, feel like Tribe. The samples were often subtle, just sitting on top of the filtered bass lines for a moment here and there. Horns stabs would whisper. Breakbeat drums would grab your neck and force it to bob your head. Nothing on the beats competed. The bass lines complemented the samples. The samples complemented the bass lines. The drums held it all together and perfectly set up Tek and Steele.

Tek & Steele were borderline perfect. Neither outshining the other, they met the beats with the right amount of energy. Tek's slightly animated voice was the counterbalance to Steele's slightly laidback voice. They wove their voices together throughout songs instead of spitting individual verses. They went back and forth in the verse and shared duties on the hook. They were just as much a unit as the beat maker duo that set them up with the lovely production.

I was inspired. Three years later, in 1998, they released their sophomore album *The Rude Awakening.* It was good, not great. Then, they went silent for 7 years. In 2005, they came out with a solid offering in *Reloaded.* But two years later, they released *The Album,* and I failed to connect with that one. Then, they teamed up with Pete Rock for a really good album, *Monumental.* But that was 8 years ago!!! They gave us an EP in 2013, but that's it. It has been nearly a decade without a proper Smif-N-Wessun album. That changed on February 22, 2019, with the release of *The All.*

The wait was well worth it, in part due to 9th Wonder and the Soul Council, who produced the entire album. Tracking in at 12 songs, *The All* is a wondrously crafted soulful Boom Bap Hip-hop album. It features elements reminiscent of *Da Shinin',* but this is far from a part two. This is a new album that stands alone all by itself.

Like their debut, the musical landscape has a very cohesive feel, as the drums, the bass, and the samples all work in unison to create fresh landscapes for Tek & Steel to till. And they do. Their energy combined with their back-and-forth rhyming style go hand in hand with the music. Plus, they are more introspective on this album than any of their previous work.

Smif-N-Wessun has come full circle. They gave us a darn near perfect album nearly 25 years ago. And in 2019, they have given us something similar. Most agree that their debut album is a solidified classic. Will we agree that *The All* is too?

THE BOOM BAP REVIEW – VOLUME 1: 2019

# CHAPTER FIVE:

## *Black Cesar* – Knowledge the Pirate
### Written by MC Till

"Black Cesar, an 18th century pirate from Africa who was described as intelligent, strong, and of immense size." These are the spoken words one hears as Black Cesar's first song, "Science Born," fades. The next song, "Mafia Codes," rings in with choppy horns, soft piano riffs, vocal samples, and Knowledge the Pirate telling street tales as only he can do. His voice is a mixture of both vulnerability and confidence. The production on the album is epic but never too much. Every sound fits just right. The music is also incredibly consistent. Every beat sounds as good or better than the one that precedes it. And the production fits Knowledge the Pirate's vocal tone and delivery. It all works and works so well.

Roc Marciano pops up early on the song "Shots Fired." This beat has two incredible vocal samples: one is very engaging and the next is luscious as heavenly angels directed by J Dilla. This beat features an engaging vocal sample followed by the most luscious vocal sample. The drums are gritty. The bass is raw. This is what east coast street Hip-hop should sound like.

But the album isn't all glim and gloom. "Time Has Come" and "Gold Bullion" both have Knowledge the Pirate sounding borderline happy. Of course, he still has his gun and drugs and life of crime. But he takes a few moments away from the anxiety of that life to just enjoy his money, clothes, and illustrious lifestyle.

Don't get too excited though. The very next song, "Darko" (produced by Roc Marciano) brings you right back to the street corner where death and destruction reign supreme. That's pretty much the overall theme of Black Cesar. However, Knowledge the Pirate seems to present that death and destruction in such a way that 1. Entertains and 2. makes the listener feel empathetic for the drug lord, the gang leader. You know this person has to make decisions that are immoral and lead to people dying or manipulated. Still, you can't help but hold the leader in high regard for living by a set of honorable principles.

I love this about art. I love when the artist takes you into the story. Knowledge does this so well. I am married and work with kids. I am as far removed from a life of street crime as one can get. And yet, there I am in the middle of it all standing next to Knowledge the Pirate himself. I see the police coming down the street. I see the young gentleman turned thug turned deceased by the hands of a cold gun turned hot. Soon, I'm the boss. I'm the one with the riches and the spoils. Then, my daughter chases my son down the hallway and, all of a sudden, I'm back to my reality.

Great art can transcend. It can create new realities or fantasies while you engage with the art. *Black Cesar* does this well in part because Knowledge the Pirate's musical ability is like the character of that original Black Pirate. It is "intelligent and strong" and its result is of "immense size" as it brings the listener into a new experience. Let's just hope we make it out!

# CHAPTER SIX:
## *Black Moon Rises* - Black Moon
## Live Listen & Review
### Written by MC Till

I've only been waiting like two decades for this! And now it is here. It is currently 5 a.m. and I'm up early with Spotify open and earphones ready. I hit play and…

"Rise of the Da Moon" opens up with their lead single, "Creep With Me." Nothing incredible here and that's okay. It is quintessential Black Moon: break beat drums, nice sample, super thick bassline, and two emcees doing their thing with laidback intensity. I like it.

As soon as the lead single ends, the booming kick of "Da Don Flow" comes right in. Again, classic Black Moon. While the kick thumps, the bassline gets funky, and subtle samples are dispersed sparingly, Buckshot spits his smooth delivery. He sounds better than ever. Apparently 5 ft. is taking a smoke break.

"Ahaaa" proceeds in a similar fashion as "Da Don Flow." This joint features one of those crunchy basslines, which sounds borderline distorted. Speaking of distortion, the mix so far is riding the fence between amateur and dope. Amateur because it does sound like they are going for pretty loud drums but are running the risk of unnecessary distortion, dope because they are going for a raw, gritty sound. So far, it is working, but they are ever so close to the edge.

Okay, I guess 5 ft. finished his spliff or whatever he was doing because, after "Pop Off" pops off with a really dope bass and horn sample, 5 ft. comes in with his signature aggressive flow. This is dope. I love hearing 5 ft. again and, like Buckshot, he sounds as good as ever with his voice sounding intense and aggressive. So, when Buckshot's' laidback voice comes in, it gives the song the perfect balance. This is definitely my favorite song so far.

"Ease Back" is more bass, break beat drums, and light sampling. Mixing it up is Method Man and General Steele who join Buckshot and 5 ft. Nothing incredible here except that it is great to hear Boot Camp Click representatives welcome a Wu-Tang member.

The Boot Camp Click's presence continues with "Impossible" as Steele remains for the second song in a row and brings Tek with him. The production on this album has settled in, and it appears it is going to remain consistently good. Not super dope, not wack. Good. Highlight of this song is hearing the transition from Buckshot into Tek. The juxtaposition of the smooth, Barry White flow of Buckshot and the higher-pitched, aggressive flows of Tek and 5 ft is beautiful. Icing on the cake is the underappreciated Steele on the hook. That guy is one of the most consistently dope emcees in Hip-hop.

"Black Moon Rise," the second single from this album, keeps the funk moving. I really enjoy the sampling on this song. Evil Dee leads the track with a stuttering sample throughout and accents it with extremely subtle keys and a very dispersed vocal sample that just jumps up really quick on the hook a few times and then lays low.

"Children of the Night" again features some subtle sampling but positioned just right with the drums. Together with another dope bassline, this track commands the head to nod back and forth. The Rockness Monster comes through for a visit on this track, and the chemistry is still there. The three Bootcamp emcees sound great together.

"Glory" opens up with the line, "When the moon turns black, everything's a wrap," and Buckshot proceeds to describe what black and black power means to him. This song seems to be the roots of Black Moon minus 5thL. Still, the song is dope Boom Bap and it is dark but also features elements of self-determination and self-power.

Next up is "General Feva," and it is another good song that keeps the album moving along. 5 Ft. is back and the beat is good. Again, nothing spectacular, it is just nice to hear the group together again.

"Look at Them" is the third single from Black Moon, and it moves slowly with laid back funk oozing at the seams.

"At Night' begins with a dope, eerie sample. The breakbeat drums drop and I can't help it. I'm sitting at my breakfast table nodding my head like it is 1994 all over again. This song isn't as good as anything they did back then, but it is still dope. As the song settles, Buckshot & 5 ft. sound like they are lurking around the corner in the middle of the night with a half moon looking over their shoulders in the midst of fog and dampening brick walls on both sides. That pretty much describes the entire album up to this point! I love the filtered bass on this song with a flickering organ sample to boot.

Okay now! "Pay Back" takes a slight left turn. It is upbeat and James Brown funky vs. dark alley muddy water puddle funky. 5

ft. is absent, but that's okay because Buckshot sounds great. His delivery is measured, riding the beat like only a legendary emcee can. He handles both the verses and the hook with a little assistance from an Erick Sermon sample. Dope.

"Roll With Me" returns Tek into the mix and welcomes 5 ft. back as well. Again, nothing incredible here. It is just a good song.

The final song, "Time Flys," might be my new favorite of the album. Everything is just right. The bassline is thick and funky as it rides around the Boom Bap drums. The sample during the hook is dope, and its presence is there during the verse, but it is filtered and in the background. This allows Buckshot and 5 ft. to shine, and they do. This is a great way to end a pretty good album.

I love a lot about this album. First, Buckshot and 5ft. sound great. Buckshot's voice is so laidback and less aggressive than usual. 5 ft.'s voice is anything but laidback. He sounds disgruntled and lets you know through the tenacity and aggression present in his voice. The two very different deliveries really balance each other out. I also love the drums and basslines. They are thick, head nodding, and funky.

What I don't love about this album is that it never really breaks out. I can't point to a single song that is not good. At the same time, I'm struggling to point out a song that just blows me away. The best way I can describe it on first listen is that *Black Moon Rises* is a good album from a great group.

What do you think?

# CHAPTER SEVEN:
## *Champion Sounds* – Wordsworth & Pearl Gates
### Written by MC Till

*"Glory,"* with its rolling snares, cloudy choir-esque vocal samples, and choppy horns opens up the album with confidence and purpose. Based on this song, *Champion Sounds* is going to be something solid. It is going to say something both musically and lyrically. Wordsworth and Pearl Gates both give solid verses with a compelling hook that holds it together. This is a good first song that wastes no time. We are into the album and so far so good.

"Glory" fades, then triumphant yet somber horns play then fade, then Pearl Gates welcomes us as a slow-moving burn of a Boom Bap beat drops. Gates flows effortlessly, weaving in and out of braggadocio and jewel swinging: "…teach youngins to show and prove. And tell the old heads the time for growth is overdo." Spuddy Roots gives us a lovely *"Champion Sound"* hook and then Wordsworth comes in and does what he does best. All other rappers beware as he channels the aura of heavyweight champs with lines like "Title contenders and rivals surrender. We drop November. You should hibernate, survive for the winter." Wordsworth is one of the greatest lyricists of all time. Case in point? Kool G Rap follows Wordsworth and kills it. Yet, Wordworth still has the better verse imo. The fact that Wordsworth has a better verse than a GOAT contender like Kool G Rap speaks volumes. Plus, Pearl Gates holds his own on this song. So, we are two songs in and already something special is happening.

We flow into *"Just When You Say"* and I can't help but think of

Jay-Z's first *Blueprint* album. That album was so dope to me because everybody liked it from kids who like pop music to the underground backpacker who just finished listening to Company Flow. That's how the beat on this "Just When You Say" track feels. It feels universal. This album is quickly warming up and showing a universal sound. The content on this track is also universal, touching on fatherhood and relationships. The adult themes here mixed with the musical landscape give the song a very mature vibe.

Wow. We are only three songs in, and we already have something special on our hands. The next song, *"Photograph,"* is somber Boom Bap at its finest. Then, we slide into "World Apart," where album producer, Quincey Tones, trades in the somber vibe for an aggressive kick-snare-bassline thumping. Minimalistic and eerie sampling provides the perfect soundbed for Gates and Wordsworth. Don't ask me what the hook says. Your guess is as good as mine. Doesn't matter because it adds to the rawness.

Okay, now it seems as if Quincey Tones tries to take a page from the new drumless formula on *"Live on Air."* However, he doesn't take all the drums out, but rather brings down the kick and snare and with very subtle high hats in the distance. Can't remember where this sample is from, but you might recognize it. He flips it in a very straightforward way, and it works. Now throw in a feature from Rasheed Chappell, and we have yet another dope joint.

*"Sincerely Yours"* brings out vulnerability, and I love it. Wordsworth and Gates offer apologetic verses. And remember when we talked about having Jay-Z appeal? Well, this song is another great example of that. The vibe is extremely cool. Lyrics

are relatable and the beat is undeniably dope, whether you like Boom Bap or not.

Talib Kweli stops by on the next song, *"These Days,"* and I can't help but think about his hit song "Get By." Both songs have a very inspirational vibe to them. Talib's hit anthem is obviously a standout banger in Hip-hop. However, "These Days" isn't too far behind. This is a well-executed song from the gospel-influenced hook to the lyrics to the lovely way Quincey Tones transitions the song from verse to hook and back to verse. Lovely joint all around.

The next three songs, *"Rollin," "Two Sides,"* and *"Like a Fool"* although very different in subject matter, all have a very similar laidback feel. One of my favorite lines on the entire album shines through on "Two Sides" where Wordsworth, talking about marital issues, says, "…now we argue about food and shoe space, stuff like who ain't put the cap on the toothpaste." If you are married or in a long-term relationship, then I know you feel this! I sure do. I love it. Real, simple, compelling. Pearl Gates continues on with some honest reflection on "Like a Fool" as he spits a nice, heartfelt verse with some really great wordplay that pulls you in from the first few lines.

"Youlogy" continues the very laidback vibes but with a very interesting twist. I'll just let you give it a listen. Let's just say, I'm thankful it is only a song.

Ironically, the last song on the album is *"First Things First."* If the first 12 songs on the album don't leaving you wanting more, this one will. It is a bit different than what you would expect from an underground, Boom Bap album, but it is a wonderful surprise. Pearl Gates trades in rapping for singing. He actually sings on a number of tracks on the album. However, he also raps on the songs. Not so much here. With *"First Things First,"* he gives us a very catchy hook and a sing-song verse. It almost sounds like something you would hear in between whoever is the hottest mainstream one-hit wonder and whoever is the next one-hit wonder. But the big difference is that this song is not a typical trendy radio-friendly single. This song, as well as the entire album, is something just about anyone can appreciate. And that is the beauty of *Champion Sound.*

Overall, this is easily one of the best albums of 2019, and I would argue it is the best album from the catalogues of both Wordsworth and Pearl Gates. If you grew up listening to Kurtis Blow and Run DMC, you will appreciate *Champion Sounds'* Hip-hop authenticity. If you grew up on Rakim, Kool G Rap, and Kane, you will appreciate the superior lyricism. If you came of age with De La Soul, Wu-Tang, and Nas, you will appreciate the 90s Boom Bap influence. And if you grew up anytime after that, I think you will appreciate the musicality of this album. The production is cohesive with Boom Bap drums and dope basslines tying it together. It also features engaging melodies and catchy hooks that open up the music to a wider audience. Great job, fellas. Hope there is a sequel in the mix.

# CHAPTER EIGHT:
## *Funhouse Mirror* - Marlon Craft
### Written by Beau Brown

When I'm not in the mood to listen to anything in particular, my fallback is always the Jay-Z Apple Music station. In a typical rotation, I'll get an assortment of East Coast Hip-hop and the occasional UGK song (I guess "Big Pimpin" figures prominently into the algorithm). It's almost a sure bet that I've heard 99% of the songs that will be played on this station, but that other 1% is where things can get interesting. I've discovered (or re-discovered) a number of artists while listening to this random assortment of music. And discovering dope Hip-hop that I haven't heard yet is one of my greatest joys in life.

This is exactly what happened when a song called "Brainiacs" was cued on my phone. The beat was good, nothing to write home about necessarily, but the lyrics and cadence grabbed me. The artist responsible for this song, Marlon Craft, sounded young and talented and hungry. On this particular song, he rapped about how it's good to stand out and be different…"Might not be on that new wave, but trust me homie, you straight, What you got on your mind is truth, and they all wearin' toupees." With lyrics like this, I needed to hear more.

I tapped "Go to Album" and found out that Craft released a project in 2017 called *Tunnel's End*. Turns out that this dude is not just a one-hit wonder. Almost every song on this release sounds dope. *Tunnel's End* really displays Marlon Craft's versatility and his beat selection skills. I remember thinking, "This sounds like classic East Coast Boom Bap, but it somehow feels modern as well." I recommend checking it out, but this article isn't really about *Tunnel's End*. It's about *Funhouse Mirror*.

After that first listen to "Brainiacs," I started following Craft on social media. He's most active on Twitter and Instagram, and he is basically writing the textbook on how to effectively use social media in this era. His posts are short, he responds to comments, and he uses video very well. Eventually, he began talking about his upcoming first album. *Wait a sec. First?! What about Tunnel's End?*

Come to find out, Marlon Craft doesn't consider *Tunnel's End* an album. This means to me that he thinks of albums as cohesive pieces of art, which I love. In my opinion, for a project to be categorized as an album, it must have a (loose) theme and a similar feel throughout. So, after a long wait, Craft finally released *Funhouse Mirror,* one of the most solid debut projects I've heard in a long time.

I'm not going to get into the track-by-track details of the album, but after listening more than a few times, here's what I came away with. *Funhouse Mirror* checks all my boxes for what makes a great album...incisive commentary on social issues (*(not) Everybody*), vulnerability (*Family*), great storytelling (*Gang S\*\*t),* lyrical dexterity and wordplay (*Word to My Mother*), and solid beats throughout (Black Milk, Statik Selektah, and others).

It's my contention that, along with artists like Joey Bada$$ and YBN Cordae, Marlon Craft is part of the next wave of Boom Bap. Whoever says young guys aren't making good Hip-hop must not have been paying attention. With albums like *Funhouse Mirror*, we get more of what Phonte would describe as, *Dope beats. Dope rhymes. What more do y'all want?*

# CHAPTER NINE
## *Holly Water* - Fly Anakin & Big Kahuna OG
### Written by Michael Stover

If you've read my Ankhlejohn *Reign Supreme* review, you already know how I feel about the DMV and the impact it's had on Hip-hop and my career in it. The Hip-hop group or collective is one of my favorite parts of Hip-hop, watching artists from different, or even shared, experiences, walks of life and talent come together to create something bigger than themselves is truly a spectacle. Nowadays, though, it feels like the group has been stripped down to simply be a business machine. Not in the case of DMV Hip-hop group Mutant Academy. A collective made up of artists, emcees, producers and the like, the roster is loaded: Fly Anakin, Henny L.O., Ewonee, Foisey, Sycho Sid, BSTFRND, Unlucky Bastards, Big Kahuna OG, Graymatter, Tuamie & Ohbliv. You don't have to be too in the loop to understand how talented this roster is, and what's more is that they're living up to that talent.

I'm off topic, though. For this review, we're focusing on Big Kahuna OG and Fly Anakin, who together are known as Big Fly. The duo have put out four EPs over the last two years and it's all culminated to their debut full-length album *Holly Water*. Press play on this and the two set us up easy for where this project is going to go, with an interview. It's a tad ironic because even Fly Anakin in this opening interview mentions Wu-Tang. Even more so, the interviewer asks what the duo speak about in their songs and after a slight pause, we're thrown into "Baggington".

Fly Anakin comes in with a slightly higher-pitched flow, but he demands your ears every time he speaks. Big Kahuna OG seems to have the confidence of 420 men, catchy with the hooks and direct with his wordplay. The duo is a match I pray we hear for years to come. Despite this being a duo affair between OG and Fly, when you look at the bigger picture, this is an all-hands-on-deck album. I'm almost certain every single Mutant Academy member makes an appearance on *Holly Water,* and I think it's fitting as, for some, this may be their first proper introduction to the team. At the end of the day, *Holly Water* is paying homage to where both artists grew up and honoring the empire they've managed to create over the last few years.

"Slimes Out" is one of a few cyphers on *Holly Water* featuring multiple emcees, in this case Duce and Monday Night (I won't be able to go into this until later, but Monday Night has quietly become one of my favorite emcees this year off guest verses alone. Please check him out.). The song produced by Hann_11 sets the stage and scene for what OG and Fly have in their hometown. Richmond, Virginia is a land of crooked cops, drug deals and a need not to fall into the system. Mutant Academy, through their chemistry and art, are actively combatting against the norms set. The last track on the album, "Boss Montage," is another unbelievable cypher that does my heart well (also ends on a Monday Night verse, just saying) with a perfect beat from Graymatter.

Believe it or not, this is music you're allowed to enjoy. They don't have to be making this huge political message to make good music. The rbchmbrs-produced "High Noon" is a chill track, and even like Kahuna says in the intro to the track, it's on some "early morning sh*t". "Shaky On The Phone" comes off as a Mutant Academy thesis statement They've been grinding and prolific almost since their inception. The duo realizes more work is required to get to the next level, and in that same breath, they understand their value. Fly Anakin opens his verse saying, "I've had one too many slices of that humble pie sh*t" and continues to wax poetic on how him and the team have gone through too much to quit grinding now. This is one I absolutely must hear live.

Going back to the reference in the introduction where the interviewer asked what they speak about in their music, I don't think the "message" is that direct. However, again when you zoom out, you must realize that these are artists who are succeeding being themselves and doing things their way. Just a few weeks before the printing of this book, we saw Fly Anakin in the studio with the one and only Madlib. Based on the output and consistency of the rest of Mutant Academy, that one picture is just the beginning of something legendary. Give *Holly Water* a spin because Mutant Academy is ready to blow up, and I'm almost certain I'll be covering this album 10 years from now for its anniversary.

# CHAPTER TEN
## *May the Lord Watch* - Little Brother
## Live Listen & Review
### Written by MC Till

*So, the morning this Little Brother album came out, I sat down and listened to it. While I listened to it, I wrote about it in real time. This is what I wrote...*

Little Brother sets off their grand return a little less grand than it could have been. Why? The absence of 9th Wonder. Everyone is thinking it. Everyone is feeling it. We miss the original Little Brother trio. However, we don't get to decide who Little Brother is. They decide. And that decision may not match our expectations, but it is not a letdown either.

Phonte & Rapper Big Pooh come back together as Little Brother and get right into with an incredibly well-mixed song, "The Feel." Just two verses and an apt hook,

"If I go too far, reel me in. Just making it real again. Tell me how to get back to the feel again." They are back and with this first song, I'm getting excited.

Following is the sorrowful announcement skit that the fictional character Percy Miracles has died. We then jump into the bouncy track, "Everything," with scattered instrumentation on top of scattered drums complete with a low-key singing hook.

"Right on Time" is another bouncy track with positivity coming from Tay and Pooh as well as the instrumental sounds. The bassline rides around the kick and snare inviting—no, demanding—the listeners nod their heads. It also features some sultry singing on the hook.

"Black Magic (Make it Better)" is next, and early in the song, you hear, "you really bout that life or are you hashtaggin?" It is so simple but so strong and challenging. This is easily my favorite track on the album so far. Tay and Pooh trade some insightful lines on this short but effective track.

"Good Morning Sunshine" is two emcees crooning over a 1,2 beat. But who or what are they talking about? They leave it somewhat vague for the listener, which I appreciate. You can take from it what you will.

I know we already stated that 9th Wonder is not present on this album, but you can hear his influence on "What I Came For." The beat is another 1-2 punch and the kick, bassline, and drums are reminiscent of 9th Wonder. So is the soulful instrumentation on top of the drums. Add Tay and Pooh, and you have a song that could sound exactly like what the trio might record in 2019. This might be my new favorite song on the album thus far. I don't know. Black Magic, although short, is really dope.

I haven't mentioned the skits much yet, and I won't say too much about them other than that they are entertaining. However, any Roots fan must know Questlove shows up on this skit, "Inside the Producer's Studio," where he introduces a guest to interview, only to find out it is the wrong guest!

I don't know who produced the next song, "Sittin Alone," but my guess is Nottz. This beat has the VA producer written all over it. The choppy drums, the stirring bassline, and the piano with synthesizer, all scream Nottz. Oh, and the fact that the beat is dope makes me think of him too. This is another feel-good song. Phonte raps, "After 35, the club is a different kind of torment." Lines like these are sprinkled throughout the album, giving it a very grown up feel, which I really appreciate. One, they are grown up. Two, I am grown up. So it works well for me. Not much in way of partying and nonsense. But the skits give the serious themes some levity.

"Picture This" might be the most cinematic song on the album thus far. The beat, although kind of laidback, also has a larger-than-life feel. The instrumentation is lush and seemingly more complex than the rest of the production, but it all works. It does not feel over-produced at all. It is just right. Then, Phonte raps, "It's soundbombing for the downtrodden." Tay might be the best at landing very simple yet very effective one-liners. And he definitely has one of my favorite voices in the world of Hip-hop.

"All in a Day" continues with the cinematic music. The instrumentation on this song is also lush over some very approachable Boom Bap drums. Phonte pretty much sums up the lyrical vibe of the album with these lines, "…memories of a different past, a different bag, in the bathroom checkin my reflection in the tempered glass. Finally accepting what I see and it's a different swag. My definition of freedom is real tight. You ask me what I'm doing tomorrow, my only response is whatever the ** I feel like." That's it - a hefty dose of self-reflection, self-confidence, and self-determination, whether we like it or not. I just happen to like it.

Oh, and we are not done just yet. "All in a Day" flows seamlessly into the final song of the album, "Work Through Me," where Phonte and Pooh spit back and forth for the last few minutes of the album. Now this might be my favorite song on the album, as I love how they tag team over the beat. I also really like the beat. It has a great soulful Hip-hop feel to it, also reminiscent of something 9th Wonder might do. But this is Little Brother without 9th, and that's okay because this is a very good album. And I'm confident this is not the last of these guys. The final line on the album is "Work through me Lord" and it is repeated a few times. Let's hope the Lord continues to work!

Overall, after one listen, I'm comfortable saying this is a really good album. Phonte and Rapper Big Pooh are excellent lyrically, spitting self-reflection and other mature themes. The production is solid from beginning to end. I think this album has mass appeal, as it should be able to attract the accolades from both underground purists and casual mainstream listeners. 9th or no 9th, Little Brother is back and they are as dope as ever.

That's how I feel. What about you?

# CHAPTER ELEVEN
## *Reign Supreme* - Ankhlejohn
### Written by Michael Stover

In my humble opinion, people have been sleeping on music coming out of the DMV (DC, Maryland and Virginia) for a long time too. I'm not a Hip-hop historian by any means, but I remember being in college listening to Diamond District's (Oddisee, XO & yU) debut album *In The Ruff* in my Ohio University dorm room thinking, "this is that good music." Fast forward to now, and we have artists like Fly Anakin, Monday Night, Ohbliv, and countless others making consistent and prolific careers out of their work. In the shadows lurks Ankhlejohn, paving his own path as a businessman and a musician.

At the absolute least, the Washington DC standout has released 10 projects over his tenure and releasing alongside some of your favorites. Multiple releases on FXCK RXP RXCXRDS that sold out in its multiple forms along with other International releases solidified Ankhlejohn as someone who's not going anywhere. While Anhklejohn continued to create and empty shelves, he was actually in the background building his own empire, Shaap Records. In 2018, he would release *The Yellow House* ,which would end up selling well. This brings us to 2019, where Ankhlejohn has been swinging for the fences all year. He's dropped a plethora of guest verses, so much so you could make a fifth 10-track album out of solely those. On top of this, he's dropped four albums. The third of those projects is *Reign Supreme*.

On July 23rd, Ankhlejohn posted a video strategically disguised

as a freestyle of him absolutely ripping a beat to shreds. Moreover, the beat sounded like some Drunken Master, Wu-Tang hotness. From the opening line, you can tell Ankh means business, but he's also constantly reflecting and studying the game and the world around him. The video and its accompanying track would become "Capital Statue" and it's by far my favorite track of the year.

All of this said, you're doing yourself a massive disservice throwing Ankhlejohn in a box. He's much bigger and working with much more than battle raps mixed with drug and gun talk. "Paid Per View" has Ankhlejohn over some lighter, retro inspired production, but between Ankh's shaap voice and enunciation, he immediately demands your respect. Tracks like "Only Fans" shows Ankhlejohn is entirely in tune with his audience and confident in what he's bringing to the table. Take it or leave it, he's going to conquer regardless.

If those tracks don't convince you of Ankhlejohn's versatility, take a listen to the three tracks after "No Battle Rap". All three of them have Ankhlejohn's heart and soul on display. Anhklejohn enjoys the game and understands his golden pen, however another loose theme throughout this project is the forthcoming of his son Reign, who the album is dedicated to. The last three tracks speak of a man matured and grown past the partying, he's focused on the bag and his incoming family. "My Opinion" puts all cards on the table and talks about where he's come from, the time it took to get clean and the impact that has. Ankhlejohn brings more to the table than "I rap better than you".....but he can do that too.

The icing on the cake of this 24-minute project is the fact that Ankhlejohn produced all of this front to back. All of these factors put together easily made this one of my favorite projects of 2019. As I'm wrapping this up, he actually just released another project, and I think I can commit to say that he's my artist of the year. Don't miss out on one of Hip-hop's best trying to lump him in with some of your other favorites. I understand the temptation to do so, but Ankhlejohn continues to separate himself with consistency and a talent that cannot be denied.

Favorite Tracks: "Capital Statue", "My Opinion"

# CHAPTER TWELVE
## *Retropolitan* – Skyzoo & Pete Rock
### Written by Beau Brown

I would venture to say that my introduction to the music of
Pete Rock was somewhat atypical. I was a high school senior
playing *NBA Street* on my Xbox when, all of a sudden, I heard
it. *It* was quite possibly the greatest Hip-hop song of all time:
"They Reminisce Over You."

Yes. Somehow, in my lifelong obsession with Hip-hop, I had
missed the legendary duo Pete Rock & CL Smooth. Chalk it up
to my younger age or the fact that I grew up in southern
Indiana, but the important thing is that it found me.

After I finished the game, I got in my car and went to the
record store. I had to dig a little bit, but thankfully, I was able to
find PR & CL's 1992 debut album *Mecca & the Soul Brother.*
Needless to say, this masterpiece was on heavy rotation for
months on end. Concurrently, I discovered InI, *Soul Surivor,*
*Petestrumentals,* and the stuff he did for Run-DMC, Nas, AZ, and
countless other artists.

For around 30 years, Pete Rock has inspired generations of fans
and artists with his soulful, jazzy, and uniquely-New-York
production. So it's pretty incredible to me that someone who
was just ten years old when *Mecca* came out has now teamed up
with PR to make another classic album.

Over the last decade, Skyzoo has become a legend in his own
right. Since releasing *The Salvation* in 2009, Sky has built an
amazing body of work, partnering with the best emcees and
producers in the game. He's positioned himself in such a way

that, when you talk about dope New York Hip-hop, you *have* to mention Skyzoo.

And that's why this new album *Retropolitan* is so monumental. In my opinion, this project defines the lineage and direction of Hip-hop. I may be overstating this, but I truly believe *Retropolitan* could be one of the most important Hip-hop albums for the next decade or more.

Rather than going into a lot of depth about the particulars of the album, I'll just share a few more reasons why I'm making such a grandiose claim.

- The album is essentially making this claim for itself, and it's believable. They open the album with a quote from the 1973 film *Gordon's War,* which tells the story of a Vietnam vet who comes back to his neighborhood and takes on the ills that have arisen while he was away. "The only ones who can make a difference are men like us," we hear the voice of Paul Winfield say. And thus we understand what this album is about...it's men like Skyzoo & Pete Rock who have the experience and skills to carry on the tradition.
- Skyzoo is the guy who finds his pocket and then spends his whole life perfecting it. He's the PhD student who dives really deeply into his subject matter and becomes a world-class scholar. He's the tennis player who develops his serve to such a flawless level that the aces just keep coming. Skyzoo isn't trying to be the most versatile rapper in the game; he knows what he does well and he's mastered it. For years to come, this needs to be the album people look to if they want to understand what being a great emcee and writing great Hip-hop songs is

all about.

- *Retropolitan* captures something that I think is very significant. Like *The Main Ingredient* and *Mecca & The Soul Brother* before it, this album symbolizes Black joy in the midst of great difficulty. In the era of Trump, there are plenty of things to lament and protest (as people should). Yet, at the same time, joy and creativity are also powerful form of resistance. There aren't too many parts of this album that feel overtly political, but Skyzoo and Pete Rock have created a sense of celebration amid the chaos. That, in itself, is a beautiful thing.

It's hard to believe there was a time when I'd never heard of Pete Rock. As a kid playing Xbox in southern Indiana, hearing "T.R.O.Y." for the first time, I had no idea how powerful of an impact he would have on my life. And now that he's solidified this connection with one of my favorite emcees, I can't wait to see what else this dynamic duo has up their sleeves.

# CHAPTER THIRTEEN
## *Sportee* – Nolan the Ninja
### Written by Michael Stover

Detroit's Nolan the Ninja exploded on the scene well before his debut album *He(art)*. However, it was the album that turned heads. Since then, Nolan has been nothing but consistent with his output while exploring with his art. I believe one facet of Nolan's game that the majority sleep on is his production. Even as I'm typing this, the Ninja dropped a four-track beat tape that I suggest listening to. Back to the topic at hand, Nolan would move on to drop *Yen* in 2017 to the same critical acclaim of his debut album. At this point, in my eyes, Nolan has solidified himself as a talent and this doesn't take into account all the singles he dropped in 2018, the beat tapes and the like. Now we have *Sportee*. Released on Mello Music Group, this is the album that marks a change in Nolan the Ninja.

When I was researching the project, looking up who did the production, I noticed that the last six tracks on the album are bonus tracks. For someone like me, seeing this album come in at 22 tracks and close to the hour mark in runtime is a dream. Especially in the case of Nolan the Ninja, where he makes the project a varied experience even when compared to his last couple albums. A prime example of this is the opening track "Oranges" which has become a viral hit so much so that Nolan has released a remix of the cut with Quelle Chris and did a COLORS performance for it in early October.

Continuing on, Nolan has something for everyone on this album, and I believe that's what makes *Sportee* so impressive. "Gems" pits Nolan the Ninja with friend and frequent collaborator A-Minus, giving fans that old school grit and grind

Nolan has become known for. All of this said, don't you dare put him in a box because with *Sportee* he's pivoting right out of it. "2 Cents" combines Nolan the Ninja with the legendary Chuck Inglish. You feel the foundation of the underground sound on the beat, but it's catchier and more accessible than just another underground track. I could imagine hearing this at the bar, and I can imagine smoking a solo blunt on a Saturday night listening to this. This type of range is what keeps the album fresh through its 22-track adventure.

Nolan has always made life music, and *Sportee* keeps that promise. We can hear Nolan's confidence continue to rise as he ascends in the industry. What shows Nolan's maturation as an artist is that he's fully aware of his rise and is moving accordingly. We get Nolan's braggadocio all over this album. His voice demands and commands your ears. However, when we step onto the latter part of the album filled with bonus tracks, we get more of Nolan's open vulnerability. "Bloom" is a beautiful track with a lighter beat and Nolan pulling back on the aggressive vocals in favor of a more deliberate and reflective approach. The last three tracks, "Hermit," "Poe," & "Felt" really put the Detroit legend's story and album into perspective.

Nolan the Ninja has yet another one with *Sportee,* as there is something for everyone on this album, and that's rare these days. It's also rare to see an album come in around an hour long and still be entertained in a climate where some artists release a lot of bloatware to run up their numbers. There's party cuts, love joints, battle raps, introspective flows and much more. If you have not given Nolan the Ninja a chance yet, here's your chance. Make sure you go back and listen to his previous material as well.

# CHAPTER FOURTEEN
## *Still* – Clear Soul Forces
### Written by Michael Stover

There's a number of Detroit releases in this book, and rightfully so. They've been creating some of the best music period for a long time now. What I absolutely love about the Detroit scene is the community and teamwork within the network. The scene supports each other, features each other and seems to be raising together. Unfortunately, I rarely see this translating to the casual audience supporting the movement in Detroit. Clear Soul Forces being the most obvious example in my humble opinion.

Clear Soul Forces is a squad of four made up of Emile Vincent (fka E-Fav), Ilajide, L.A.Z and Noveliss, each with their own distinct style and flavor. Now listen, I'm willing to admit I was late to the party. I missed their debut tapes and their debut album. However, when *Fab Five* dropped, it brought me back to the days of growing up on Hip-hop albums. Hearing four new voices and wondering the origins and what else these four had created was invigorating. These were four brand new artists with entire catalogs and careers behind them, features, videos and more that I hadn't heard or seen yet. *Fab Five* is easily one of my favorite albums, and I wholly believe CSF doesn't get the credit they deserve for that album and their follow-up *Still*.

Four years later, here we are, we finally get a follow-up to the critically acclaimed *Fab Five* in *Still*. To be frank, I had big expectations going into this. Since 2015, Noveliss has ascended into one of Hip-hop's most prolific emcees. Ilajide has dropped four different projects, both in beat tapes and raps (while producing the majority of it). While we don't hear from Emile Vincent or L.A.Z as much as I would like, both put out projects this year worth checking out.

That's more background than usual for a review. However, I think it's all important and necessary information to help you understand the statement that *Still* makes. First things first, this is not *Fab Five,* and I don't believe they were trying to replicate *Fab Five* in *Still*'s creation. Ilajide is stepping up here and taking the helm producing and engineering the entirety of *Still* (with "Diamond Rhymin'" being the exception).

The minute *Still* explodes into your earpiece with "Blaow," the squad hasn't skipped a beat. Again, each emcee demands your attention, Noveliss with his stoic yet sword like bars, Ilajide sounds like he's flowing through time and space when he raps, the laidback yet killer style of L.A.Z combined with Emile Vincent's booming delivery makes for a unique listening experience. With all four emcees being such distinct talents in their own right, you're certain to walk away from this or any of their projects with a favorite or multiple favorite emcees from the group.

*Still* winds up being a testament to everything the group has accomplished and gone through up to this point. Clear Soul Forces is STILL dope, CSF is STILL creating some of the best group Hip-hop music today, and it's time we give them the credit they deserve. Clear Soul Forces album *Still* came out towards the beginning of the year, but in my opinion, they had one of the best first-quarter releases of 2019. If you enjoy hearing emcees murder beats with the chemistry of the Golden State Warriors, *Still* is a must listen.

Part Three

# RETROSPECTIVES

# CHAPTER FIFTEEN
## 30 Years Later:
## A Look Back at *3 Feet High & Rising*
### Written by MC Till

I remember it clearly. I was at my cousin's house in Indianapolis when I saw it. I saw, for the first time, a copy of *3 Feet High & Rising* by De La Soul. It was on cassette, and I wanted it badly! Somehow, I had a blank cassette tape with me. I'm not sure if other kids my age carried blank cassettes on them or if I was just a spazz for the music, but regardless, I was equipped. My cousin began the recording process for me. I didn't realize it then, but I was about to get a bootleg copy of what would become the most influential album in my life.

There was an unforeseen problem, one I would not realize at the time but shocked me with surprise later. My immediate family was from Evansville, IN, and it was almost time to leave. So, my cousin only had time to record the first side of the album for me. I didn't realize there was even a second side...until later. I bumped the heaven out of Side A of that album and loved it! So, when I later realized there was another half to the album, I was so, so excited. And that second side was just as good if not better than the first!!!

This album was and is not just a collection of songs. It is an adventure with skits! Oh, the skits! My goodness, the skits were so fun and quirky. As far as I know, De La Soul was the first to utilize skits on such a wide scale. It wasn't just an intro skit or interlude skit. They had skits all over the place. Songs were skits. They told me who had dandruff and who needed to take off different played-out pieces of clothing. My personal favorite was telling me who needed a luden due to bad breath.

And then there is the actual music. Wow, the rapping on that album wasn't like anything I'd ever heard. It was like stylish talking. They could say so much with so little. They were not wordy and overcomplicated. And they were not simple either. They were nobody else. They were De La Soul, and they had incredible production too. Similar to the rapping, the beats were so different. The sampling on that album is eclectic and groundbreaking. It was funky and jazzy, soulful and weird. The music overall felt just right.

Sure, I had heard and enjoyed artists like Slick Rick, the Beastie Boys, Run D.M.C, Public Enemy, L.L. Cool J, and others. But it was *3 Feet High & Rising* by De La Soul that grabbed me, slapped me in the face, and said, "this is what you will pursue for the rest of your life." I hadn't even been on this planet for a full decade, and I already knew who I was. I was a Hip-hopper.

And 30 years later, I still am. Hats off to De La Soul for classic, groundbreaking music that has inspired so many!

Now, please excuse me as I go back to listen to Side A of *3 Feet High And Rising*.


Peace,

MC Till

# CHAPTER SIXTEEN
## 25 Years Later: A Look Back at *Resurrection*
### Written by MC Till

I remember the moment clearly. My dad had just finished vacuuming the living room. I walked in, turned on Rap City. Just then, my grandpa walked through the door. We were having some sort of family event that day. As my dad's dad sat down on the couch, the video to Common's "Resurrection" appeared on the screen. The beat, produced by No I.D, featured a very jazzy piano sample. That's what did it. That was the moment jazz and Hip-hop united two seemingly distant generations together.

My grandpa was pretty old then. He would soon have dementia. He might have had a mild case of it already. Yet, when he heard that jazzy piano loop, he recognized it. He was an avid jazz listener. He had an old Zenith record player. Above the player, nailed to the wall, were all of his grandkids. When we went over to Grandma and Grandpa's house, he would sometimes be sitting there listening to jazz while looking at his grandchildren.

I will always cherish that moment when he sat down on the couch with me that day and listened to one of my favorite rappers. He didn't judge it like many people from his generation. He listened to it and found something to appreciate. He enjoyed the jazzy influence. I enjoyed that too. And that day, we sat there and enjoyed it together.

Now, that was probably the only song he ever heard from Common. I, on the other hand, listened to every single song on that *Resurrection* album. And today, I've listened to every single Common song ever! If you know of some obscure B-side or remix song, please let me know. I love Common, and it all started with that seminal album, *Resurrection*. That album is Hip-hop perfection.

No I.D. produced the entire album, and he deserves as much credit for this gem as Common. The music is incredible. No I.D. utilizes breakbeat drums flawlessly. Every drum sequence grabs your head and demands it nod back and forth. His use of sampling is also immaculate. Each sample fits the drums just right. He didn't overproduce a thing. The room that No I.D. provides for Common is perfect.

And Common doesn't slouch. He tells stories. He brags. He rhymes just for the sake of rhyming. He does it all and does it with so much style. His ping pong delivery captivates. It invites you to follow along. The beats are engaging. The rhymes and the delivery are engaging. It is one of Hip-hop's finest moments.

Common is good at that, creating moments for people to cherish forever. He provided a moment like that for my grandpa and I. Just recently, he provided another such moment for me with his new album *Let Love*. On that album, Common jumps into a song all about his failings as a father. The song is slow. The drums meander around the piano that must have been dusted off from sitting in a heavenly trunk in some abandoned attic. And there is Common with all his style pouring his heart into the song. He tries to justify himself to his daughter, stating all the things he did for her. She responds with, "It's the things that you didn't do." Man, that hit me. I have a daughter and a son, and I know firsthand that the greatest gift I can give them is my loving presence. That moment in his song hit me. It stopped me in my tracks and reminded me. It was like Common was there in the room talking directly to me.

Common has been doing that now for over 25 years! His catalog is vast and is one of the best in music. He gave us *Resurrection* over two decades ago, but he continues to give us transformative moments.

When I see the music videos my kids watch, I remember that transformative moment with my grandpa. That Hip-hop song from Common was not his music. It was mine. Still, my grandpa found something positive, just as I try to do with my kids. May these moments of coming together be ever more common (ooooh, see what I did there! Okay, kind of corny. But, still.)

# CHAPTER SEVENTEEN
## 15 Years Later:
## A Look Back at *The College Dropout*
### Written by Beau Brown

Like many Hip-hop fans these days, I'm conflicted. I'm conflicted about a lot of things, but the thing that seems to conflict me the most is what I'll call "The Kanye Situation" (or TKS for short). TKS is quite complex, but I would say the basic components of this phenomenon are as follows:

(1) *His recent musical output.* Don't get me wrong. I liked several parts of *Life of Pablo* and a couple songs on *Kids See Ghosts.* But *Jesus Is King* was a total flop. In fact, it was painful to listen to at times. All that to say, my general impression is that Kanye's most musically creative years are behind him.

(2) *His public persona.* I know. I know. This has always been a thing with Kanye. He's always been brash and arrogant. He's always been an open book, it seems. Yet, I think the difference up until recently is that Mr. West was egotistical and self-revealing in a kinda lovable way. For the past few years, though, it just seems like he's been working out his private issues in public. I'm certainly not shaming him for being open about his mental health (and I can only imagine how fame and fortune has exacerbated any pre-existing issues), but in my experience, being in the spotlight while battling with personal demons is not good for anyone.

(3) *His politics and theology.* I don't think I need to say anything more about this.

That's TKS. So why spill any more ink about it? TKS has been written and talked about and covered from every angle. In general, I think many Hip-hop heads have written him off completely. Well, I'm writing about Kanye West because *College Dropout* is one of my favorite albums of all time, of any genre--- and it just turned 15 years old.

In the early aughts, when popular Hip-hop was being dominated by club bangers and dirty south anthems, this guy from Chicago sporting a pink polo showed up and started making soul-infused, sample-heavy, heartfelt Hip-hop. And instead of dismissing him as some sort of weird backpacker, people loved Kanye.

It probably didn't hurt to have Jay-Z's marketing muscle behind him, but nonetheless, this was a genuinely talented Hip-hop artist making dope music. His drums were so dusty, his samples were just perfect, and he could actually rap well. He talked about materialism, racial justice, and education in a way that really resonated. He helped bring Common and Talib Kweli and Mos Def and others to the attention of a much larger group of people. Kanye was checking all the boxes for me.

Throughout 2004 and every year since, I have consistently bumped *The College Dropout.* I think I might even have the whole album memorized. Songs like "Two Words," "Jesus Walks," "All Falls Down," and "Through the Wire" are permanently embedded in my psyche. I couldn't forget them if I wanted to.

This is the root of my conflict. TKS has put such a bad taste in my mouth that I can't listen to his music anymore. Every time I think of him wearing that MAGA hat in the Oval Office, every time I catch a clip of one of those ridiculous "Sunday Service" things, every time I see a pair of Yeezys, every time I hear

THE BOOM BAP REVIEW – VOLUME 1: 2019

someone try to convince me *JIK* is a good album…I get more and more frustrated.

Listening to *The College Dropout* is just a painful reminder of how far the mighty one has fallen. At this point, I can't deal with the cognitive dissonance. My brain can't process the journey between the lyrics, "And I basically know now, we get racially profiled, 'Cuffed up and hosed down, pimped up and ho'd down" and the statement, "When you hear about slavery for 400 years … For 400 years? That sounds like a choice." Now, I know people progress (or regress) in their thinking, but this is just too far of a bridge to cross.

Of course, I'm not suggesting that everyone should feel the way I do. There are certainly folks who will be able to compartmentalize the various aspects of Kanye's historical artistry and personality. Just as there are many people who love *Million Dollar Baby* but dislike Clint Eastwood's politics, it's conceivable to think of *College Dropout* as a single work of art that should be considered (and enjoyed) apart from anything else.

Here's the rub, though. Hip-hop is a unique form of creativity, in that there has always been an immediate connection between artist and art. What I mean is that the average person can take in a piece of architecture or a painting without knowing anything about the creator(s). Obviously, one's appreciation will increase after learning more about the artist, but that will require additional resources. In Hip-hop, however, the accumulation of language builds a stronger sense of unity between messenger and message. And the highly verbal nature of the music means that the voice of the artist will create a reciprocal relationship between public statements and artistic catalog.

This is not just to pick on Kanye, either. It becomes increasingly difficult (for me, at least) to consume any Hip-hop created by a rapper who is publicly homophobic, misogynistic, or just inane. For example, I love Action Bronson's artistry, but some of the things he's posted on Instagram make it difficult for me to enjoy his music. And even though he has somewhat apologized for saying transphobic things, I still associate his voice with a strain of intolerance that makes me very uncomfortable.

My point is that the voice of a Hip-hop artist carries a lot of weight. And when that voice becomes intertwined with objectionable ideas or bad music, it ripples throughout their entire body of work. For Kanye, the reverberations of the last couple years have perhaps permanently displaced my ability to take delight in *The College Dropout*.

So, this finally raises the question: Is it still a classic? My knee-jerk response is yes. Just because I can't personally enjoy a piece of art does not make it any less of a masterpiece. Kanye's debut album is still a great piece of work. The beats are incredible. The songs are memorable. The lyrics are on point. The guest appearances are all dope. It's just a really really good project. It's a classic! Yet, for the time being, it's a classic I cannot enjoy.

I wish Kanye the best, and I appreciate what he's done in and for Hip-hop. I look forward to the day when I can bump this album without the residue of "The Kanye Situation" sitting in the front of my mind. Given how quickly he seems to shift his perspective, that could be sooner than I think. Until then, there's plenty of other great Hip-hop to enjoy.

# CHAPTER EIGHTEEN
## 10 Years Later:
## A Look Back at *Modern Marvels*
### Written by Michael Stover

Let me just get this out of the way: Theory Hazit is my personal favorite emcee of all time. In my opinion, front to back, his discography is flawless and is a healthy blend of personal anecdotes and straight up filthy emceeing. I won't go into extreme details, but about 10 years ago, Theory was coming off his LP release *Lord Fire* (my favorite album of all time), and my assumption was we wouldn't be hearing from the Cincinnati legend for a long time. I remember being in college listening to the Sphere of Hip-hop Podcast/Radio Show, and Illect Recordings had a commercial for a brand new Theory Hazit album. This was different though. It wasn't exactly the Boom Bap, grimy production we were used to. The production was cleaner, had more glamour and even a touch of space age sound to it. Theory Hazit and producer Toni Shift would release their collaborative LP *Modern Marvels* in December of 2009.

This was the first album I went all in for, grabbed the deluxe preorder, fit with CD, the instrumentals and a bonus project. Anyway, popping in the album, you're immediately met with a grandiose beat seemingly from the future. Theory Hazit again continues to show that he can hop on damn near any beat and make it his own. I'm not even going to pretend to understand the creation process, but when you take into consideration that he released a full-length a year before this, dropped *Lord Fire 2* alongside *Modern Marvels,* and produced Sareem Poems' *Black and Read All Over* album for Mello Music Group, I'm not sure how he was able to create *Modern Marvels.*

With the new production Toni Shift provided here, Theory Hazit decides to conduct some experiments of his own. "Hands In Hi-Fi" grabbed me in the commercial I heard, and hearing the full track was heavenly. The track features Cincinnati artist and friend Wonder Brown and Portugal singer Aletta. The chemistry and blend between the four is unmatched, and I wish they were a group because I could listen to this all day. The next track, "Marvelust," has Toni Shift going deeper into the space funk sounds, and Theory Hazit sounds right at home.

Theory Hazit is clearly a talent, but what I love about how he creates and the music he releases is that he's not afraid to work and collaborate with others. Lightheaded (Braille, Ohmega Watts and Ozay Moore fka Othello), Wildchild, DJ Idull, MotionPlus, JustMe and more. One of the standout tracks on the album, "It's So Sweet," features Visionaries member and prolific legend LMNO. Another perfect match on this one. In fact, the duo of LMNO and Theory Hazit would go on to release their own album together called *Determined To Fly.* Theory Hazit also gave us a "hidden track" in a way. If you take a look at "Uncanny," there are no other guests mentioned in the tracklist, but Theory came through and brought Lady Luck, Ill Poetic, DonWill, Cas Metah, MotionPlus and others to the track. A pleasant surprise I feel most artists don't take advantage of these days.

It's easy to listen to Theory Hazit and understand that he's a top tier emcee. It almost seems too easy for him sometimes. However, what makes Theory Hazit my personal favorite emcee of all time are the emotional tones that he touches on throughout his records. One of Theory's first singles when he stepped onto the scene was "I Just Wanna Go Home," and the brutal honesty of his past will immediately grip the listener. Since that release, Theory Hazit has continuously opened his heart up and been vulnerable with his audience. *Modern Marvels* is no exception. "Concealed Sorrow" is one of the best songs I've heard. I've cried to the track, and if you go back and search for the official single, there's a remix adding another emotional dimension to the track. I won't spoil anything here, but I strongly suggest giving it a spin. "Late Summer Sun" is a beautiful song where Theory pays homage to those that helped and raised him.

*Modern Marvels* is a classic to me, an underrated one at that. Toni Shift brings production that is still ahead of its time today. I'm confident Theory Hazit can rhyme over any kind of production. While there's nothing wrong with the dusty, grimy Boom Bap we know and love, there are plenty of artists experimenting with the sound and it's more than worth checking out. Now, if I'm remembering correctly, Theory Hazit & Toni Shift are a duo together called "Modern Marvels." While its been a long time, I hope that we can get a sequel to this album one day.

# CHAPTER NINETEEN
## 10 Years Later:
## A Look Back at *Sojournalism*
#### Written by Michael Stover

You may or may not have heard of Sojourn, but he's one of the OGs coming up in Hip-hop in the 90s. The influence he's had on Hip-hop still holds true today. However, there's a curious case about Sojourn. The album I'm writing about here, *Sojournalism: The Summer Chronicles,* is the only album we've gotten from the California standout in his now-over-30-year tenure. The idea of a Sojourn album was a myth back in the 2000s. I was introduced to him through Surreal's single "A Car and A Job". Walk with me here as I wasn't truly shown Hip-hop til about 10th grade. Before that, TI's "Rubberband Man" was all I thought existed. Sojourn's verse on "A Car and A Job" eventually had me frantically searching the Internet to find more music to no avail. Eventually, I learned the California legend was a part of a group Future Shock, which was a part of an even bigger group called The Tunnel Rats. To speed the story up, Sojourn remained prolific, dropping guest verses on a number of projects but still never releasing a solo album. Eventually, through Braille's label Hip Hop Is Music, Sojourn would release his debut album *Sojournalism: The Summer Chronicles.*

This album stands as Sojourn's thesis or testament in my eyes, especially now that we're ten years out. Before you even press play on the record, look at the tracklist. We get features from Surreal, Sivion, Theory Hazit, BlameOne, and other heavy-hitting names. A step further, the production credits are also filled with insane names, OhNo, PNS from the Molemen, Dert, S1 and even Sojourn himself all had a hand on this record. Even a decade ago, my expectations for this were high and Sojourn smashed it out of the park and stands the test of time especially now.

Coming in at just under an hour, Sojourn gives you plenty to think about, while remaining true to the Hip-hop culture that he represents. One of my favorite assets of underground Hip-hop albums back in the 2000s was I felt we got a more eclectic mix of music. A record would have a good portion of tracks prioritizing lyrical ability and then, towards the end of the record, we would see a more vulnerable and open side of the artist. If you read the previous chapter, you see that Theory Hazit & Toni Shift's *Modern Marvels* fits this as well. We get a proper introduction from Sojourn with production by Supreme Keys, and he sets the table for the Chronicles and journey we're about to go on.

"Art Verses Commerce" has Sojourn aware of the expectations this album has, while sticking to being himself and expressing that on this album. Ruslan from The Breax comes through with my favorite instrumental on the album—jazzy, funky, even now, I wish I had the instrumental of this. The next track, "Fool's Gold," goes into detail about our world's obsession with money and how it's fostered toxicity amongst ourselves and our relationships. Again, with Sojourn, it is about waxing poetic, but also imparting some wisdom and sense into the listener.

Don't get it twisted, this is in no way a preachy album. In fact, I'd go as far as to call Sojourn a Renaissance Man of Hip-hop. "Human Resources" is a perfect example of this, where we don't get a single word from Sojourn. In fact, Mass Reality's Big Rec handles all the vocals, and Sojourn is in the background beatboxing. For me personally, I still to this day haven't seen anyone do this on an album, and I don't know why. The way Big Rec rides the beat as Sojourn changes the tempo on him is nothing short of a spectacle. I remember playing this a million times on my first few listens of this album. This is only one instance of Sojourn really paying homage to the Hip-hop culture. If you keep listening after the record is "finished," we get a bonus track featuring Ahred from Future Shock and then Propaganda and Raphi of Tunnel Rats/Foot Soldiers(?). I actually remember hearing this track on a Foot Soldiers mixtape but never knew the official name. Easter eggs and callbacks like this are just another facet that makes Sojourn one of the best we have.

As I said earlier, what brings albums like these full circle are the real and human elements that allow us to relate to the artist. The entire second half of this album embodies this. "Definitely Special" is a romantic cut, talking about the beauty of love and finding your soulmate. "The Craving" and "Civil War" talk about the harsh and brutal battles we all have within. One of my other favorites, "Road Less Traveled," has Sojourn bringing his Future Shock crew back together along with Blame One to really open the wound of how difficult that road is.

Between the raw poeticism and delivery to the big names that show up on the album, Sojourn's debut and only album is a masterpiece. With Hip-hop, while the base criteria is being a good emcee and showing you know how to rap, I believe what marks a great emcee is showing those vulnerabilities to your audience. *Sojournalism* gave me a lot to think about as a young college freshman venturing out into the open world for the first time at 19 years old. The album hits differently and with more understanding, as I turn 29 next month heading into 30. Thinking about having my own family, understanding the music industry and my career path in it, the constant call for growth as a Black man and hopefully future father was sparked heavily during this release.

We still get guest tracks from Sojourn, but I do hope one day we get a proper follow-up to his debut. I'd love to know what he's been up to since the last issue of *Sojournalism* rolled out.

# CHAPTER TWENTY
## 10 Years Later: A Look Back at *Brooklynati*
### Written by Michael Stover

In 2005, classic Hip-hop group Little Brother released their sophomore album *The Minstrel Show* to critical acclaim. I think we all can make the argument that they're one of the best groups to exist. If you go back and listen to the album again, you can catch Tanya Morgan's Von Pea and DonWill on a few of the interludes ("Cheatin" & "Slow It Down"). I bring this up because, to me, in listening to their sophomore effort *Brooklynati,* it evokes some of the vibes that *The Minstrel Show* has. This review isn't about Little Brother though. Tanya Morgan, at the time of *Brooklynati*'s release, was a trio made of DonWill, Von Pea & Ilyas. Tanya Morgan is a piece of the powerhouse group The Lessondary too. In my opinion, *Brooklynati* was the group's breakout album, and it easily stands the test of time today.

Tanya Morgan is a force of a group and shows versatility and utter talent on this album. The chemistry is unmatched. It's like watching Lebron, Dwyane Wade & Chris Bosh play together in album form. We don't just get three "dope" emcees rapping a 16 with a hook and passing it to the next guy. No, there's clear planning and song creation here. From the jump, *Brooklynati* starts with "On Our Way" and has DonWill opening the track with a beautifully sung and melodic hook. The Hip-hop group is one of my favorite facets of the culture these days, and Tanya Morgan nails the embodiment of creating as one. Von Pea, DonWill and Ilyas all bring their own style and humor to the table.

All the production is done in-house by either Von Pea or Lessondary partner-in-crime Brickbeats, with one beat from Aeon. There's a mix of genres here, a dash of soul, a dash of jazz, R&B, even hardcore if you want to get technical, and Tanya Morgan nails all the notes. In my humble opinion, every single track on here is incredible and exercises versatility. As we head to the center of the album, the humor shines in "Dont U Holla". We're all struggling out here, there's no need to holla if you aren't trying to pay up. Von Pea's first speaks on the frustrations they've had to deal with as a group with venue owners believing Tanya Morgan is a singer. Despite the trio being veterans in the Hip-hop space, they're still forced to pay dues and deal with disrespect.

*Brooklynati* is a fictional place combining Brooklyn, New York and Cincinnati, Ohio. They flesh out the fictional city with skits and interludes. Usually, I'm not a fan of either unless done correctly. Thankfully, Tanya Morgan has them placed perfectly, and each one adds context to the world building of Brooklynati. Just before the "Interlude," we get "Plan B," which might be my favorite track on here as it accomplishes the world building of Brooklynati while also telling a story that I feel gets overlooked in the world of independent music. There's a lot to risk when you step into the artist space and no guarantee of success. The Brickbeats-produced track mixed with the wonderfully-sung hook adds the variety that keeps *Brooklynati* such an intriguing listen even now. Ilyas also comes through with one of my favorite verses ever really putting into perspective what kind of difference each one of us makes in each other's lives without thinking about it. Tanya Morgan may be a group of three, but they are one.

The last half of the album gives us backbreaker after backbreaker of hits and a gang of features from some of your favorites. After the "Intermission," we get features from the entire Lessondary crew in "Never 2ndary". This affirmed in my mind that we needed a Lessondary album as soon as possible (and we would get that album in 2016). The second half also gives us features from Phonte, Blu, Kay, Carlitta Durand and more. "We're Fly" is a track I didn't appreciate fully until years later, but I think it fits the mold of an ideal second to last track. Produced by Von Pea, it has that heavenly, chill feel with a soulful hook and verses from the team. Surely at this point, you see how fly Tanya Morgan is.

"Brooklynati" is a classic and perfect album in my opinion. Front to back, from the raps to the production, there are no misses here. With the amount of features on here, you would think the voice of the group would get lost sometimes. Not the case here. Each feature feels like a genuine guest to the city of Brooklynati, but at the end of the day, Tanya Morgan runs the city and it shines through all 15 tracks. As I continue to reflect on this album, the more thankful I am that DonWill's verse on Theory Hazit's "Uncanny" grabbed me so much to research the group. Tanya Morgan is horrifically underrated, in my opinion. They've been creating next-level music for over a decade now. Get hip and take a trip to *Brooklynati* and make sure you thank them later.

# OUTRO

Here we are. 100+ albums later. We listed our favorite Boom Bap albums of the year and wrote about many of them. We offered you our opinions and you read all about them. We cannot begin to tell you how thankful we are for you. Of course, true artists make art because it is within them. However, don't let an artist fool you. We love to be acknowledged. We love when people listen to or read our work. We like to be taken seriously and appreciated for our contributions. You took the time to read our words throughout this book and for that, we are forever grateful.

We are also forever curious, and we care what people think. So, if you have a top 10 or 15 or 20 or 100 list from 2019, we would absolutely love to see it. If you are a writer or would like to become a writer, we would love to read what you think about your favorite albums this year. We told you ours so if you want to tell us yours, that would be awesome. Just hit us up. If you would like to join Everybody's Hip-hop Label, simply head over to everybodyshiphop.com

Before we sign off until next year, we do want to once again send a huge THANK YOU to all our Patreon members at Everybody's Hip-hop Label, both past and present. You believe in the vision of building up community around the creation, distribution, and discussion of quality Hip-hop music. We would not have been able to pull off this book if not for you. Thank you for believing in us. Thank you for supporting us. You are the best.

| | |
|---|---|
| Akshay Wadekar | Joey Taylor |
| Andrew Whitton | John Stickney |
| Angelo Santoro | Kenyon Turner |
| Brent A. Miller | Kiff Kilpatrick |
| Carlos Castillo | Mark Mcauley |
| David Annett | Matthew Phillips |
| Dee.kay | Michael Charron |
| Derrick Braziel | Myrtis Smith |
| Dhaval Kale | Nick Palermo |
| Elizabeth Koontz | Robert Campbell |
| Eric Hansen | Spicey Ky |
| Jarrod Alberich | Taylor Hogle |
| Jay Whyle | Who Izzy |
| Joe Thomas | |

Peace and love to you all.

MC Till
Michael Stover
Beau Brown